THE YOUNG TRAVELER'S JOURNAL & ACTIVITY BOOK

A fun, action-packed workbook to help you explore, adventure and remember it all!

This book is dedicated to the Mommy Poppins community— the passionate parents who create thousands of articles, event listings and guides to help families have amazing adventures together—and our equally passionate readers who use them.
We'd also like to thank our family, and favorite travel buddies, Edward, James and Arthur.

Table of Contents

Activities and Games

Get the most fun imaginable out of your trips.
If you want to dive straight in, go for it!

GAMES

Hello, Adventurer!

You're about to set off on some big adventures!
Traveling is a chance to try new things, taste lots of yummy foods, meet new friends and go to cool places.

This book will help you turn trips into adventures by noticing the awesome things around you and keeping track of all the amazing things you do! Plus, it's packed with ideas to make your travels more fun.

WHAT IS A BUCKET LIST?

Some people have a list of places they dream about visiting or things they want to try over the course of their lives, which is called a bucket list. You could have a bucket list of foods you want to eat, places you want to go or things you want to do.

How to Use This Book

This journal is divided into 15 adventures. Any time you're heading off on a trip, pick a matching section. For longer trips, you may fill out many adventures along the way! There are even Everyday Adventures to help turn regular outing into fun-filled days too.

Make sure to check off the Travel Badges you earn as you go. You'll find them near the end of the book, along with a Souvenir Spot to keep memories.

What are you waiting for? Let's go!

Want some fun travel inspiration? Find hundreds of travel guides with the best stuff for kids on *MommyPoppins.com*.

Adventure Bucket List

As you complete your trips, come back to this page and check off everything you've done!

	ADVENTURE	LOCATION
✓	**Take a road trip**	
✓	**Fly in a plane**	
✓	**Stay in a hotel**	
✓	**See a landmark**	
✓	**Visit a city**	
✓	**Visit a museum**	
✓	**Explore nature**	
✓	**Go to the beach**	
✓	**Eat in a restaurant**	

Everyday Adventures

Turn a normal outing into an adventure with these activities!

	ADVENTURE	LOCATION
✓	Go to the market	
✓	Fun with friends	
✓	Neighborhood adventure	
✓	Family time	
✓	At the park	
✓	Movie night	

My Bucket List

What other adventures do you dream of? Add your bucket list items and check them off the list when you get to do them!

	YOUR ADVENTURE	LOCATION
✓		
✓		
✓		
✓		

About You!

Name: ....

Age: ....

A fun fact about me:

....   **Draw your face!**

....

....

....

....

PORTRAIT OF AN ADVENTURER

➤ Where do you come from?

➤ What is the best adventure you've been on?

➤ Circle the words that match the kind of adventurer you want to be. You can even add your own words to the list!

funny   creative   bold   smart   clever   fast   strong

brave   good at climbing   outdoorsy   thoughtful

friendly   kind

How does traveling make you feel?

It's OK to feel excited, nervous, happy, sad or all of the above. Circle your feelings below.

EXCITED

BORED

UNSURE

CURIOUS

HAPPY

BE READY!

Adventures can be bumpy. Our plans might change, we might not have our favorite foods or things might get messy. But that's OK! Part of being a good adventurer is learning to be ready for anything. Sometimes, surprises turn out to be the best parts of our trips!

LOVED

SURPRISED

FRUSTRATED

AFRAID

Preparation Station

You're about to set off on your next adventure. You're sure to see, do and experience lots of cool new things. A little planning helps make your trip extra fun. Before you get going, take some time to ensure you're ready for adventure.

DATE

Where are you going?

. . . .

Have you been there before?

. . . .

Write down three things you look forward to doing or seeing on this adventure.

1. ....

2. ....

3. ....

Is there anything you're worried about?

....

....

....

....

Tomorrow, you'll be somewhere new!
Write down where you'll be in the morning,
afternoon and when you go to bed.

Morning: ....

Afternoon: ....

Bedtime: ....

Color in the arrow on the scale below to rate how excited you are for this trip!

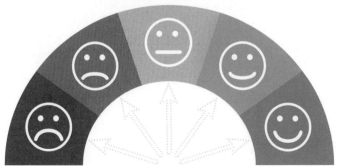

Pre-Trip Checklist

Getting ready for a trip can be an adventure of its own! Don't wait until the last minute to pack. Use the checklist below to make sure you bring everything you might need.

✓	Check the weather. Do you need to prepare for rain or chilly nights?
✓	Think about where you'll be. Do you need a swimsuit, sneakers or a fancy outfit?
✓	Choose outfits for each day. Remember to bring extra socks and underwear!
✓	Wear comfortable shoes.
✓	Pack yummy snacks for the road.
✓	Bring things to do, like books, small toys, games and this journal!
✓	Keep all your fun stuff in a small backpack so that you have it handy.
✓	Bring a water bottle.
✓	Don't forget your toothbrush!

Packing in the Fun

Smart travelers pack light with things they'll use over and over. How many of these handy things can you draw in the suitcase before you run out of room? Tuck a few into your bag, too!

- Spiral sketch pad
- Pencils, crayons or markers
- Stickers or a sticker book
- Deck of cards
- Small travel games
- One or two books
- Small toys

Five Things to Do With a Piece of Paper

With just a pen and a piece of paper, you can have a blast anytime, anywhere.

1. Dots and Squares

Draw a grid of dots. You can make your grid as big as you want, but three dots across and three dots down is a good way to start. To play, each player uses a different color pencil to take a turn drawing a line between two dots. No diagonal lines allowed! If your line completes a square, put your initials in the square and go again. When the board is full, whoever has claimed the most squares wins.

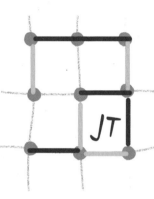

2. Creative Creatures

Fold a piece of paper into three sections. Draw the head and neck of your creature in the top section, then fold it back so it is hidden and pass it to the next person. They will draw the body and arms in the second section and pass it back with the last blank section face up. Draw the legs and feet in the bottom section. Unfold to reveal the creature you created together!

3. Stickman

One player thinks of a secret word and draws blank lines for each letter of the word. The other player tries to guess the word one letter at a time. If they guess a letter correctly, write the letter where it goes in the word. If the letter is not in the word, draw one part of a stick figure, like the head, body or arm. Try to guess the word before the stick figure is completed!

4. Got Your Back

One player thinks of an animal or object and draws it (on paper) on another player's back. If the player can guess the word in 60 seconds, they win!

5. Mini Book Making

Fold a piece of paper in half the long way. Unfold it and fold it in half the other way, then fold it in half again in the same direction. Unfold that fold so it's still folded in half and cut or rip along the crease from the top of your fold, only to the crease in the middle. Open the paper and then refold it the long way. Push the two ends together so that the middle sections pop out, making your paper look like a plus sign from the top. Fold the two outside pages forward and you have a book! Can you make a storybook about your trip?

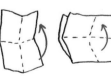

| Fold in half, unfold and then fold the other way. | Fold in half again, up from bottom. | Unfold halfway and cut or tear from crease to fold. | Refold long way and push ends together. | Fold end pages around to make a book! |

What's the Plan?

It can be helpful to know the plan before you even leave the house. Plus, you'll have extra time to get excited about the cool stuff you'll be doing. Write down what you'll be doing on each day!

DAY 1:
Where will you be?

. . . .

What will you do?

. . . .

. . . .

DAY 2:
Where will you be?

. . . .

What will you do?

. . . .

. . . .

DAY 3:
Where will you be?

. . . .

What will you do?

. . . .

. . . .

YOUR TRIP BY THE NUMBERS

Although you can't directly measure the fun you'll have and the memories you'll make, it's interesting to break down your trip in numbers!

Number of days: ☐

Number of meals you'll eat: ☐

Number of beds you'll sleep in: ☐

Number of hours to get there: ☐

Number of times you'll brush your teeth: ☐

What's on Your Mind?

It's normal to have a lot of thoughts and feelings before an adventure. You might be excited to experience new things or wish you could stay home instead. Use this space to write or draw everything that's on your mind right now.

ADVENTURE 2:
LET'S HIT THE ROAD!

Take a Road Trip

The great thing about road trips is the freedom to stop wherever you'd like! There are so many exciting things to see and do along the way.

DESTINATION:

Who are you traveling with?

What are some things you hope you'll see on your trip?

What did you bring to keep busy on the road?

Make a playlist for your trip. What songs do you want to listen to?

. . . .

. . . .

. . . .

. . . .

Think of a joke to make the other people in the car laugh. Write it here, then tell it and write down everyone's reactions.

. . . .

. . . .

. . . .

. . . .

. . . .

. . . .

WOULD YOU GO?   ☐ YES   ☐ NO

One of the largest roadside attractions in the world is the Big Lobster in the Limestone Coast region of Australia. Inspired by American roadside attractions, this crustacean—named Larry—is 55 feet tall. That's about as tall as a five-story building!

welcome to
The Big
Lobster

Map It Out!

Draw a symbol and label for each place you plan
to stop. Then connect them all with a road.

YOUR HOME

DRAW YOUR DESTINATION

Road Trip Bingo

Can you get four in a row by keeping your eyes out the window?

bridge	windmill	mountain	police car
stop sign	gas station	airplane	cow
tractor	red car	bicycle	barn
silo	diner	road work	truck

Are We There Yet?

With a little road trip math, you'll never have to ask that question again.

Ask your driver how many miles until you reach your destination and how fast you are going. Divide the number of miles you still have to go by the speed you are going to find out how many hours are left in the trip.

Miles left	÷	Speed (in miles per hour)	=	Hours to destination
Miles		Miles per hour		Hours

PIT STOP PLAY

After sitting in the car, it's a good idea to get your wiggles out when you can finally stretch your legs. Have a dance party, see who can do the most jumping jacks or play follow the leader with hopping, skipping and silly walking.

Road Trip Word Search

See if you can find all of the travel-related terms hidden in the puzzle below. (They can be vertical, horizontal, diagonal or backwards!)

R	T	H	I	A	L	T	C	M	A	B	D
A	O	N	I	P	Q	I	A	Y	E	J	R
D	U	K	H	G	F	V	R	E	V	Q	A
I	R	D	G	F	H	G	P	Y	J	N	O
O	I	N	A	S	R	W	R	V	Z	U	B
O	S	R	P	O	U	P	A	U	A	M	L
K	T	A	B	N	R	I	M	Y	V	F	L
T	Q	F	T	L	E	B	T	A	E	S	I
V	A	C	A	T	I	O	N	C	P	X	B
M	B	E	N	O	V	E	R	P	A	S	S
E	L	C	Y	C	R	O	T	O	M	S	H
E	R	U	T	N	E	V	D	A	Y	G	E

ADVENTURE   CAR   MOTORCYCLE   ROAD   TOURIST
BEEP   HIGHWAY   OVERPASS   SEATBELT   TRAFFIC
BILLBOARD   MAP   RADIO   SUITCASE   VACATION

Answers on pg. 27

Road Trip Games

Spending time in the car with loved ones can be half the fun! Here are some fun games you can play on the road.

1. Freeze Dance

Turn on some tunes and have a seated (and seat belted) dance party. Have one person turn the music off suddenly and everyone has to freeze in whatever silly position they were caught in. Take turns as the DJ!

2. My Cows

Driving by farm after farm? Try this: When you see cows out the window, say "My cows!" as fast as you can. Then quickly count the number of cows you see. Those cows are added to your collection. When you pass a graveyard, whoever says "Bury your cows" first gets to erase another player's cows. Whoever has the most cows when you reach your destination wins!

3. Twenty Questions

Keep them guessing with this classic game! Choose anything you can think of and announce whether it's an animal, plant or mineral. Next, everyone asks you yes-or-no questions until they've narrowed down what's on your mind. If they guess correctly before the 20th question, they win!

4. The Name Game

You'll have to dig deep to win this game. Start by saying any name, like "Rachel." The next person will need to come up with a name that starts with the last letter of the name you just said. So if you said "Rachel," the next person could say "Logan," and so on. You're out when you can't think of a name that starts with the right letter. You can also play this game with the names of places.

5. The Alphabet Game

This game can be played by yourself or with others. Keep your eyes peeled during the drive and try to find each letter of the alphabet in order, starting with "A." You might see letters on billboards, license plates or road signs. When you get all the way to "Z," try to do it backward!

Answer for the word search on pg. 25

See more road trip games on MommyPoppins.com.

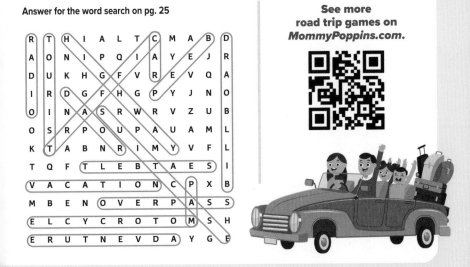

You Have Arrived!

Now that you're a road trip expert, it's time to record what you thought about your journey.

What was the strangest thing you saw?

....

....

What was the best thing you ate on the road?

....

....

Rank your pit stops from best to worst!

BEST 1. ....

2. ....

3. ....

4. ....

WORST 5. ....

THE JOURNEY IS THE REWARD...OR IS IT?

This famous expression teaches us to enjoy traveling, not just arriving at the destination. What was more fun on your trip: the stops and time in the car together or what you did at your destination? Explain why.

Take to the Skies

3-2-1, liftoff! Planes are a great way to travel long distances quickly. You can take a plane almost anywhere in the world!

DATE

Where are you going?

. . . .

Who are you traveling with?

. . . .

Is this your first time on a plane?

. . . .

How long is your flight? . . . . **hour(s)** . . . . **minute(s)**

Do you have to switch planes to get to your destination? If so, where will you stop?

. . . .

. . . .

. . . .

If you could fly anywhere in the world, where would you go?

. . . .

. . . .

. . . .

What are you looking forward to about your plane ride?

. . . .

. . . .

. . . .

DOODLE SPOT!

Draw your own flying machine! Does it have wings like a duck or propellers like a helicopter? Where do the passengers sit? What noise does it make while it flies around?

Pre-Flight Fun

Check out these neat activities you can do before you board the plane.

1. Airport yoga

Being cooped up on a plane isn't always super comfy. Before your flight (or between flights if you're going somewhere that requires more than one plane), try a little airport yoga! Find a spot that's out of the way and stretch your body with a simple yoga routine, like the one on the right. How does your body feel different after stretching? See which poses you can do!

2. Suitcase rainbow

This game makes you pay close attention to all the suitcases around you! Sit at a gate and watch all the travelers walking by with their bags. Look for a suitcase of each color of the rainbow, starting with red. Whoever spots red, orange, yellow, green, blue, indigo *and* violet suitcases first wins! You can also try this game with purses or backpacks, sunglasses, hats or any other item you can think of.

How many of each color can you find?

red	
orange	
yellow	
green	
blue	
indigo	
violet	
pink	
white	
black	

3. Take a walk

An airport is kind of like its own town—a town where there's a lot of fast food and everyone carries a suitcase. If you have time before your flight, try taking a walk with your grown-up and seeing the sights! Many airports have art galleries, play areas, restaurants and sometimes even museums that you can visit without even leaving the building!

Draw or list the most interesting things you saw on your walk on the blank spot above.

4. Takeoff jumping jacks

Watching planes take off and land can be fun, but you can add another layer to the game by challenging yourself to do five jumping jacks for every plane you see take off out the window. How many jumping jacks were you able to do? Can you touch your toes every time you see a plane land?

Airport Alphabet Game

Make walking through the airport more fun, whether you're heading toward your gate or wandering around while you wait for your flight. Keep an eye on the shop signs, arrivals/departures boards or anywhere else you see words. Try to find one word starting with each letter of the alphabet. If you have a family member who wants to play, divide up the alphabet or turn it into a race!

A

B

C

D

E

F

G

H

I

J

K
....

L
....

M
....

N
....

O
....

P
....

Q
....

R
....

S
....

T
....

U
....

V
....

W
....

X
....

Y
....

Z
....

What's Out the Window?

Looking out of the window on a plane can be exciting. You might see farms, the ocean, cities or lots and lots of clouds. Draw what you see.

Draw what you think you'd see out of these unique windows!

YOUR BEDROOM

SPACESHIP

CASTLE

SUBMARINE

In-Flight Poetry

Use the magazine in your seat pocket to get some poetic inspiration. Look through the magazine and collect 10 words you find interesting, funny or beautiful in the box below. Then, use those words to write a poem! It can be about your trip, your destination or anything you want!

Airplane Scavenger Hunt

It might seem like there isn't much to see on a plane, but look around you! Can you spot these things?

- Someone with their shoes off
- A flight attendant
- A can of tomato juice
- Someone watching an animated movie
- Someone sleeping
- Someone wearing headphones
- A cloud shaped like an animal
- A (hopefully empty) barf bag
- A backpack

Rate Your Trip

Color in how many stars you would give
your plane ride in each category.

BUMPINESS

GREAT LANDING

DELICIOUS SNACKS

GOOD VIEWS

☆ ☆ ☆ ☆ ☆

COMFY SEAT

☆ ☆ ☆ ☆ ☆

OVERALL RATING

☆ ☆ ☆ ☆ ☆

You've Landed!

Reflect on your journey through the skies.

What was your favorite part of the plane ride?

....

....

....

What was your least favorite part?

....

....

....

What did you do on the flight?

....

....

....

Were you able to get comfy or sleep?

....

....

What snacks did you eat?

....

....

What are you going to do now that you've landed?

....

....

....

....

What advice would you give others about flying on an airplane?

....

....

....

WOULD YOU GO?
☐ YES ☐ NO

Singapore's Changi Airport might be the coolest airport in the world. It has a 130-foot indoor waterfall, a four story slide, a tropical rain forest, a butterfly garden, plus attractions like a hedge maze, bounce nets, and lots more!

Staying in a Hotel

Staying in a hotel can be an adventure of its own. From check-in to checkout, it's fun to explore a home away from home!

DATE

Where are you?

. . . .

Who are you traveling with?

. . . .

What is the name of the place you are staying?

. . . .

If you were in charge, what would you name the hotel?

. . . .

Are you near or far from home?

....

How long would it take you to drive home?

....

How long would it take you to walk home?

....

**Imagine that aliens have just landed on Earth
and they're knocking on the door of your hotel room!
How would you explain to them what a hotel is?**

....
....
....
....
....

Hotel Scavenger Hunt

Different hotels have special items tucked around that you might not know about unless you look for them. Explore your hotel with your adult to see how many of these things you can find.

Swimming pool	
Ice machine	
Breakfast buffet	
Elevators	
Mini fridge	
Mini shampoo and conditioner	
Free coffee	
Slippers	
Fake plants	
Gym	
Iron	

Circle the thing you would most like to bring home with you if you could.

Lobby Stories

Sometimes, it can be fun to see all the different people staying at your hotel.
Try doing some people-watching next time you're in the lobby or eating breakfast at the hotel restaurant. Everyone has their own story!
When you see someone interesting, make up your own story about what their life might be like.

What is their name?

....

**What do they do
for work?**

....

**Why are they staying
at the hotel?**

....

....

Where are they from?

....

**What are they
going to do today?**

....

....

....

**Draw a sketch of
your chosen subject.**

Would You Go?

At Atlantis The Royal, a hotel in Dubai,
you can ride 105 water slides, surf in a wave pool,
swim with sharks or paddle with dolphins.

On the other side of the world, Sanctuary
Treehouse Resort in Tennessee has 130 treehouse
rooms and suites you can stay in, complete
with secret hatches, swings and giant slides!

Which resort would you rather visit? Why?

. . . .

. . . .

. . . .

**What would your
dream hotel be like?
The sky's the limit!**

. . . .

. . . .

. . . .

. . . .

. . . .

. . . .

. . . .

**Draw what it
would look like.**

Star Power

Did you know hotel star ratings are not just opinions? Hotels must offer certain things to earn their stars. For instance, a two-star hotel must have free shampoo and soap, but to earn five stars, they have to be fancy brands.
A three-star hotel needs to have a shower with a tub, but a five-star hotel should have a jacuzzi tub and fancy bathrobes in each room.

What fancy things would you make hotels do to earn five stars?

. . . .

. . . .

. . . .

. . . .

. . . .

. . . .

APPRECIATION STATION

Small acts of kindness can make a big difference! Write a thank you note to some of the hotel helpers who have made your stay nicer.

Checking Out Checklist

Having a checking out checklist helps
make sure nothing gets left behind.
Search all these spots and see if you can be
a hotel room hero by finding any forgotten items!

UNDER THE BEDS
Do you see any missing items?

BATHROOM
Did you pack your toothbrush?

OUTLETS
Did anyone forget a charger?

IN THE BED COVERS
Is there anything tangled in the sheets?

CLOSETS OR DRAWERS
Did anyone leave their shoes, jackets or underwear?

SAFE AND FRIDGE
Does your room have these?
Did you put anything in there?

No Sock Left Behind!

Help the sock make it into the suitcase before you head home! For bonus points, set a timer and see how fast you can solve the maze without doubling back.

Answer on pg. 55

ROOM SERVICE

One extra special thing about staying in a hotel is ordering room service. At some hotels, you can have any food off the menu delivered right to your room! If you could order anything in the world and have it show up in your hotel room right now, what would you order?

Games to Play When You Can't Fall Asleep

These bedtime activities will have you snoozing in no time (and they're much more fun than counting sheep).

1. Rhyme Time

Choose a word from the list below, then think of as many rhyming words as you can. You can also play with a partner. Take turns giving a word for the other person to rhyme.

Cruise	**Hike**	**Lake**	**Tour**
Drive	**Jet**	**Pack**	**Tram**
Fly	**Map**	**Sea**	**Zoo**

BONUS: Write a poem that uses all the rhymes you came up with!

2. Jump-athon

Jumping on a hotel bed (shoes off) is kind of a tradition. Challenge yourself to keep going until you're really tired.

3. A to Zzzzzz

This word game is surprisingly good at lulling you right to sleep. Choose a category, like fruit or animals. Then, try to think of one thing in that category for each letter of the alphabet, starting with A. Bet you can't make it all the way to Z without drifting off!

Dream Journal

How much time do you spend thinking about your dreams after you wake up? Did you know that some people keep a diary about every single dream they have? Try it out! You might learn something about what's going on inside your head!

Date:

What did you dream about?

Draw a picture of your dream.

All Packed Up and Ready to Go

Think about what made your stay an adventure.

What's the best thing about staying in a hotel?

. . . .

. . . .

. . . .

Would you want to live in a hotel all the time? Why or why not?

. . . .

. . . .

. . . .

What's the funniest thing that happened on this trip?

. . . .

. . . .

Staying in a hotel can be nice, but what are you looking forward to doing when you get home?

. . . .

. . . .

. . . .

Acrostic Accommodations

An acrostic poem describes a person or place using words that spell out their name. Can you write an acrostic poem that explains your feelings about staying in a hotel?

H ....

O ....

T ....

E ....

L ....

Answer for the maze on pg. 51

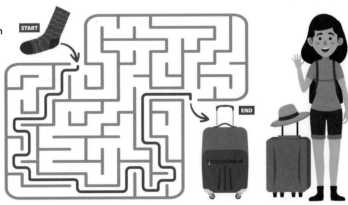

See a Landmark

Landmarks are places that lots of people travel for miles and miles to see. They might be natural wonders, amazing human-made creations or places where historical events took place. Use this page to describe the landmark you are visiting in as much detail as you can.

DATE

What landmark are you visiting?

. . . .

Who are you traveling with?

. . . .

What type of landmark is it: a natural landmark, building or other structure, historical place or something else?

. . . .

Write down the story of the landmark.
Why is it famous or what is it known for?

. . . .

. . . .

. . . .

It's exciting to see something new. You might wonder what it will be like when you get there. What questions do you have about the landmark you are about to see?

- . . . .

- . . . .

- . . . .

- . . . .

- . . . .

- . . . .

WOULD YOU GO?   ☐ YES   ☐ NO

Off the coast of Australia, the Great Barrier Reef is the largest collection of coral reefs in the world. Imagine a giant, colorful, underwater city for fish, turtles and other sea creatures. To visit the Great Barrier Reef, many people go scuba diving, but this natural wonder is so big you can even see it from outer space!

Make Your Mark

Imagine a landmark dedicated to someone in your life!

What event or achievement would the landmark honor?

....

Describe your landmark.

....

....

Write the plaque that would go next to the landmark. Describe what your landmark celebrates and why it is important.

....

....

....

Draw what you want your landmark to look like. Before you get started, ask yourself: How does the design help show what the landmark is for?

Know Your Landmarks

See if you can correctly name the famous sights in the pictures below.

1. The Eiffel Tower ....

2. The Great Wall of China ....

3. The Taj Mahal ....

4. The Colosseum ....

5. Machu Picchu ....

6. The Great Pyramid of Giza ....

7. The Statue of Liberty ....

Answers on pg. 61

Stamp It

Design your own postcard so you'll always
remember your landmark adventure!
Draw the landmark on the front of the postcard.
Make sure to include yourself in the picture!

Who do you want to send your postcard to? Use the back of the postcard to tell them all about what you saw!

Design your own stamp!

POSTCARD

Bonus points if you find a real postcard and send it to your bestie!

FIVE THINGS TO WRITE ON A TRAVEL POSTCARD

A postcard is a classic way to tell people at home that you are thinking of them while you are away. Since the note area is small, it's easy to dash one off and send it to a friend. Here are ideas of what to write:

- A funny story that happened on your trip
- Something delicious you ate
- A fun fact you learned
- What you are seeing right now
- The best thing you've done so far

pg. 59 answers
1. F, **2.** C,
3. A, **4.** E,
5. D, **6.** G, **7.** B

Would You Rather

Below are some of the most visited and least visited landmarks in the world.

World's Most Visited Landmarks
➤ Times Square, USA
Located in New York City and known as the heart of Broadway, this commercial intersection is filled with big billboards and bright lights, street performers and crowds of people. Times Square receives 250,000 to 300,000 visitors every single day.

Times Square, USA

➤ The Eiffel Tower, France
The Eiffel Tower was built over 100 years ago in Paris, France! It was supposed to be temporary, but it became so popular that the city decided to keep it forever. There are long lines to visit the top of the tower and look out at the whole city. At night, the Eiffel Tower lights up with lots of sparkly lights.

Eiffel Tower, France

➤ The Forbidden City, China
A palace complex that was formerly home to China's emperors, the Forbidden City in Beijing is made up of impressive buildings filled with beautiful antiques, like thrones and royal riches. On a tour, you'll hear many tales about the royalty who lived there.

Forbidden City, China

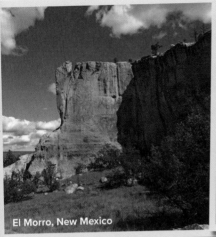
El Morro, New Mexico

Shibam, Yemen

World's Least Visited Landmarks

➤ El Morro, USA

One of the least visited landmarks in the United States is El Morro in New Mexico, a national monument that preserves a prehistoric pueblo (village). For hundreds of years Spanish explorers, American pioneers and others stopped here and carved their names or messages next to ancient Native American carvings. Their additions might be some of the oldest graffiti in the U.S.

➤ Shibam, Yemen

Rising out of the desert, this 16th-century city is made of mud brick high-rise buildings that are 4 to 11 stories high, making them the oldest skyscrapers in the world. In fact, Shibam is called "the Manhattan of the Desert"!

If you had to choose, which attractions would you most like to see? Rank them!

1. . . . .   2. . . . .   3. . . . .

4. . . . .   5. . . . .

You've Seen the Sights!

Reflect on the time you spent observing natural or human-made wonders.

What new facts did you learn about the landmark you visited?

What was the most interesting thing about your landmark?

What is one other landmark you'd like to see? How is it similar or different from the one you saw on this trip?

Overall, would you recommend this attraction to a friend? Why or why not?

Landmark Review

Fill in the scales ranging from low to high
to match your experience!

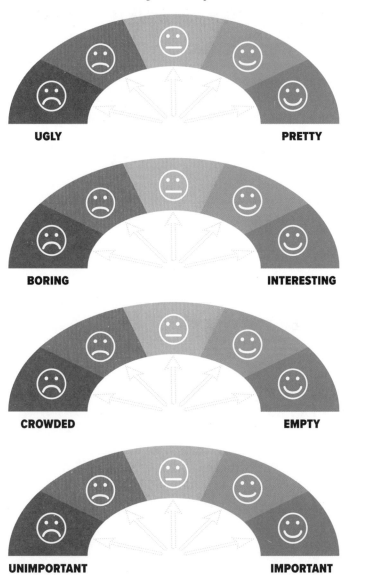

UGLY — PRETTY

BORING — INTERESTING

CROWDED — EMPTY

UNIMPORTANT — IMPORTANT

Visiting the City

The hustle and bustle of a big city is always exciting.
There is so much to do, see and explore!

Where are you?

....

Who are you traveling with?

....

Which part of this adventure are you the most excited about?

....

....

How is this city different from where you live?

....

....

Design Your Own Souvenir T-Shirt

Souvenirs are a great way to remember your travels when you're back home. You might see magnets, key chains and even T-shirts with a city's name on them, like the famous I ♥ NY shirt. Try designing your own souvenir T-shirt for the place you're visiting!

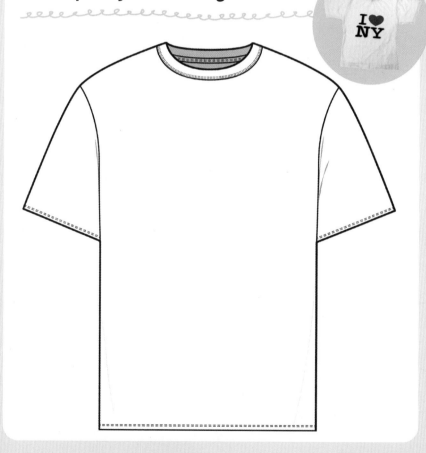

Five Things to Do in the City

Now it's your turn to be a city guide!
Work together with your adventuring group to
figure out the best places to visit in the city.
Think about what will be the most fun and interesting
as well as what everyone in the group will enjoy.

1. Visit a museum

Which museum will you visit?

_____

_____

_____

Why did you choose this museum?

_____

_____

_____

2. See a landmark

Which landmark will you see?

_____

_____

What are other landmarks you'd like to see if you have time?

_____

_____

_____

_____

4. Visit a park
Which park will you visit?

_____
_____
_____
_____

What fun things will you do in the park?

_____
_____
_____
_____
_____
_____

3. Explore a neighborhood
What will you do there?

_____
_____
_____

What are you most excited to see?

_____
_____
_____
_____

5. Eat in a restaurant
Which restaurant will you try?

_____
_____
_____

What foods are you excited to eat?

_____
_____
_____
_____
_____
_____

After your city tour, reflect on all the things you did.

Which one would you recommend to a friend?

_____
_____
_____
_____
_____
_____
_____
_____

A Street by Any Other Name...

You can learn a lot about the history and culture of a city from what each street is called. You may notice that the names are really similar, or different, to your hometown!

Did you know Main Street is the most common street name in the United States? In France, the most common street name is Rue de l'Église, which means Church Street.

Can you find Main Street in the city you're visiting? What about Church Street? What do you see there?

. . . .

. . . .

. . . .

What do you think the second and third most common street names are?

. . . .

. . . .

. . . .

Usually, Main Street is the busiest street in a city. Draw, color and name what shops and activities you would put on your Main Street if you were in charge.

MAIN STREET

Games for Waiting in Line

You'll reach the front of the line before you know it with these fun activities.

1. Finger Puppets

No puppets, no problem! Using a pen or marker, draw faces or characters on each of your fingertips. It can be fun to make each face fit a theme, like the characters from a fairy tale, or give each face its own personality. When you're done, use your finger puppets to put on a puppet show!

2. Mirror Me!

Stand face-to-face with the other player. Choose one person to be the leader. The leader makes slow movements, while the follower tries to copy the movements like a reflection in a mirror. Try to be as in sync as possible! If you have more than two people in your group, you can choose one leader and everyone else can try to follow along!

3. Gibberish Theater

Try having a conversation without any words at all. Communicate by only speaking gibberish and using your hands, arms, legs or facial expressions to get your point across. You can agree on a topic beforehand or keep it a surprise. At the end, it's fun to have the players reveal what they were really trying to say.

4. Fortunately, Unfortunately

This game is all about drama! Work together as a group to tell a story about the luckiest and most tragic made-up character. Start by describing your character and then take turns describing the ups and downs they face while in the city. One person will say, "Fortunately..." followed by something good. Then, the next person starts with "Unfortunately..." and the story will take a turn for the worse.

5. One-Word Story

Work together as a group to tell a story...but you can only add one word at a time! Take turns adding a single word to the story and see where the tale goes!

Sensational Senses

We use the five senses to learn
about the world around us.
What did your senses tell you about the city?

I saw:

I heard:

I smelled:

I tasted:

I touched:

MAKE IT MAKE SENSE!

In this game, you'll use your senses to guess the identity of secret items. To play, choose one person to be the item-master. Everyone else will be guessers. The item-master will secretly put several items into a bag.

You can use a shopping bag or whatever you have handy, but make sure no one can see the items through the bag! The guessers must reach into the bag and try to guess what the items are using only their sense of touch.

Transit Time

Big cities have buses, trains, trams, trolleys or ferries to help move lots of people around efficiently and reduce pollution and traffic jams. Did you take public transportation on your trip?

Write down what types of transit you took and what you thought of them.

Can you help the bus get to its destination?

Answer on pg. 78

You Don't Say!

When you travel to a different place, people may speak a completely different language. Sometimes, even when they speak the same language, they may use different vocabulary and pronunciations or use words differently. This is called a dialect.

Dialects can show us how different cultures and communities talk. They can also help us learn more about the history and diversity of our world!

ANY WAY YOU SLICE IT

One example of regional dialects is what people in different areas of the U.S. call a submarine sandwich, also called a sub in many places!

➤ Can you match the word to the region?

1 Hero
2 Hoagie
3 Po'boy
4 Grinder
5 Dagwood

a Minneapolis
b New Orleans
c New York
d Boston
e Philadelphia

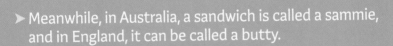

➤ Meanwhile, in Australia, a sandwich is called a sammie, and in England, it can be called a butty.

➤ What's your favorite kind of sandwich?

Answers on pg. 79

What new words did you learn on this trip?

....

....

....

Write a conversation between two people who live in the place you are visiting. What types of things might be important to them?

A: ....

B: ....

A: ....

B: ....

A: ....

B: ....

A: ....

B: ....

A: ....

B: ....

A: ....

You're a City Expert

Reflect on your travels (and possibly plan your next trip!) in the prompts below.

How did your urban adventure make you feel?

- ☐ Excited
- ☐ Happy
- ☐ Nervous
- ☐ Tired
- ☐ Bored
- ☐ Curious

What was the best thing you did in the city?

. . . .

. . . .

. . . .

. . . .

. . . .

. . . .

Answer for the maze on pg. 75

What's a funny thing that happened on this trip?

· ·

· ·

Do you want to return? Why or why not?

· ·

· ·

What do you want to do next time you visit this city?

· ·

· ·

**Are there other cities on your bucket list?
Write down a city you want to visit and why.**

· ·

· ·

· ·

**Draw your favorite skyscraper, building
or park that you saw on your trip!**

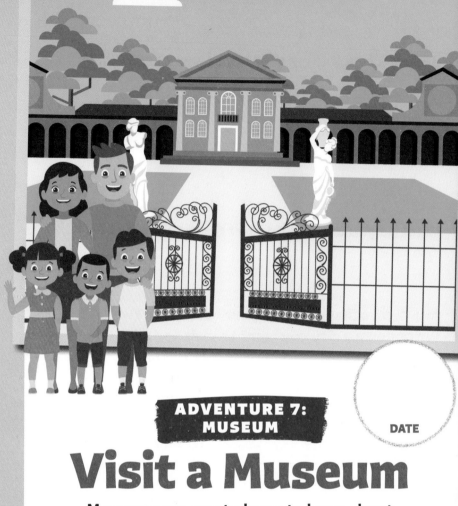

DATE

Visit a Museum

Museums are great places to learn about things that make you curious.

What museum are you visiting?

....

Who are you with?

....

....

What type of museum are you visiting?

☐ Art   ☐ Children's

☐ History   ☐ Natural history

☐ Science

☐ Something else ....

What is something you are curious to learn about at the museum today?

....

....

....

Sometimes, museum buildings used to be something else, like a palace or a warehouse. Other museums had special buildings built just for them. Can you uncover the history of this museum?

....

....

....

What clues do you have?

- ....

- ....

- ....

➤ Located in New York City, MoMA PS1 was originally an unused 19th-century public school building.

Tips for a Kidtastic Museum Trip

These activities will help you get the most out of your visit.

➤ **Make a scavenger hunt** of the things you want to see at the museum. Can you find them all during your visit?

➤ **Check the website** for any special family workshops or performances.

➤ **Stop at the information desk** when you arrive. Many museums have kid guides or activity packs to make your visit more fun.

➤ **Try an audio guide.** This is a fun way to explore a museum with headphones on. You never know what you might learn!

DOG SPOTTING

Spice up your museum trip by turning it into a secret dog spotting mission! Keep your eyes peeled for dogs throughout your visit. From paintings of dogs to fossils of their ancient ancestors, how many dogs can you find? If dogs aren't your thing, try looking for something else, like cats, birds, dragons or unicorns! You can even assign everyone in your group a different animal to look for and see who finds the most.

Museum Manners

Do you know your museum manners? Circle the things that are usually allowed at museums and cross out on the things you should definitely not do.

C asking questions

D yelling

A eating a snack

B touching the art

E running

F walking

G whispering

H playing hide and seek

I sketching

J taking notes

K lying down

Answers on pg. 85

Gorgeous Gallery

As you walk through a museum, you'll notice things that you think are cool, pretty or interesting. You might also see things you don't like at all! Choose your favorite pieces and draw them in the frames below to make your own gallery with all your favorites!

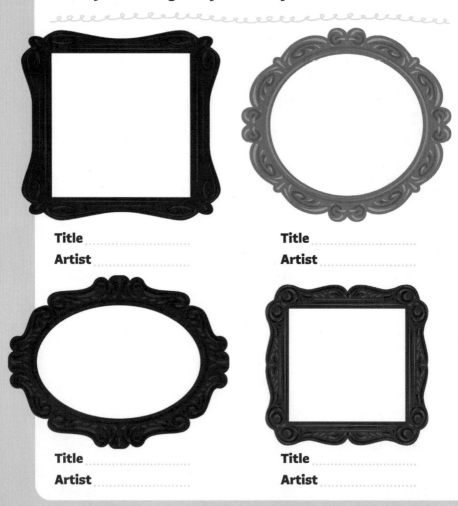

Title

Artist

Title

Artist

Title

Artist

Title

Artist

What is your absolute favorite thing you've seen at the museum? Draw it in the frame below!

What is it called?

. . . .

Who made it?

. . . .

What year was it made?

. . . .

What do you like about it?

. . . .
. . . .

MEDIUM MADNESS

You can find many kinds of art in a museum. From paintings to sculptures and beyond, it's amazing to see what people can make. Try to find one of each during your visit!

- ☒ **Painting**
- ☒ **Drawing**
- ☒ **Photograph**
- ☒ **Sculpture**

pg. 83 answers:
DOs: C, F, G, I, J **DON'Ts:** A, B, D, E, H, K

The YOUseum

Museums are dedicated to things that we care about and find important. What if there was a museum all about you?

**What kind of museum would you have?
It could be devoted to science, art, or even something specific, like stickers!**

. . . .

. . . .

What would your museum be called?

. . . .

Write your own biography to be displayed in the museum. What are the most important things visitors should know?

. . . .

. . . .

. . . .

List the objects you would put on display that tell the story of who you are. Draw them below.

- . . . .
- . . . .
- . . . .

- . . . .
- . . . .
- . . . .

- . . . .
- . . . .
- . . . .

WOULD YOU GO?
☐ YES ☐ NO

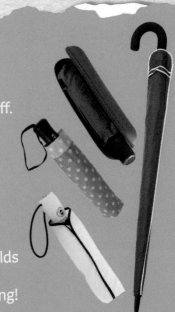

When you think of museums, you might think about giant buildings full of old stuff. But there are hundreds and hundreds of tiny, unique museums scattered all over the world!

The Umbrella Cover Museum in Maine is dedicated entirely to collecting and displaying the little sleeves that hold umbrellas. This quirky museum is on an island you can only reach by ferry and holds hundreds of different umbrella covers. The museum even has its own theme song!

Superlative Search

Can you find these extreme items around the museum? Try playing with someone else in your group and compare your findings at the end!

The oldest object:

The heaviest:

The grossest:

The prettiest:

Something that would taste the worst if you licked it:

The most expensive:

The object from the farthest distance away:

The most boring:

The loudest:

The scariest:

The silliest:

TAKE-HOME DAYDREAM

➤ If you could take home one item
you saw on display today, what would it be?

. . . .

➤ Why did you choose that item?

. . . .
. . . .
. . . .

➤ What would you do with it?

. . . .
. . . .

Museum Passport

There are so many kinds of museums to explore! Every time you visit a museum on your travels, fill out one passport stamp. See if you can you fill your whole passport!

INTERNATIONAL PASSPORT

Type	Country Code	Passport No.
Surname		Personal No.
Given Names		Sex
Date of Birth		
Date of Issue		Holder's Signature
Date of Expiry		

Draw your face!

You're a Museum Explorer!

Consider what items, artists, historical figures and fun facts intrigued you the most.

What is the most interesting fact you learned?

What do you think you will remember most about this museum?

What was the strangest thing you saw?

What did you enjoy the most?

What did the museum make you think about?

. . . .

. . . .

Who do you want to tell about this museum?
What would you tell them?

. . . .

. . . .

INSPIRATION STATION

Seeing all the amazing things at a museum can be a great source of inspiration. Inspiration is what makes you excited to create your own art, come up with inventions or write your own story. Use the box below to write about or draw one thing that inspired you today.

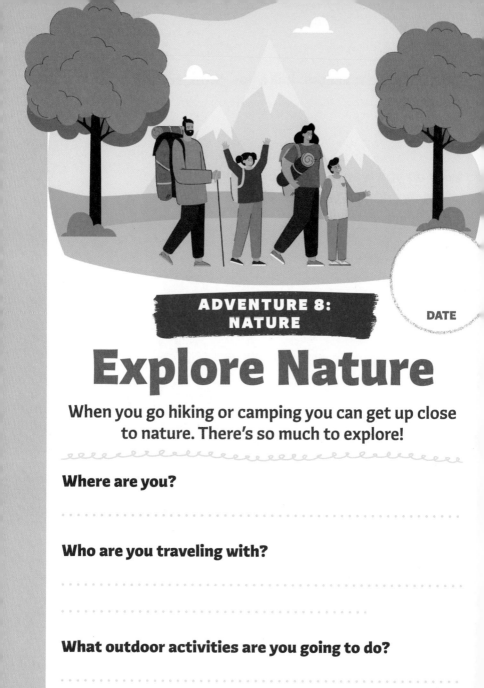

ADVENTURE 8: NATURE

DATE

Explore Nature

When you go hiking or camping you can get up close to nature. There's so much to explore!

Where are you?

....

Who are you traveling with?

....

....

What outdoor activities are you going to do?

....

....

....

Learn about where you are going! Write down three plants and three animals you might see there.

➤ **PLANTS**

1. . . . .

2. . . . .

3. . . . .

➤ **ANIMALS**

1. . . . .

2. . . . .

3. . . . .

Where are you staying?

☐ Camper

☐ Cabin

☐ Tent

MOTEL

☐ Motel

WOULD YOU GO?
☐ **YES**   ☐ **NO**

The Grand Canyon receives about 5 million visitors per year. Created by millions of years of the Colorado River wearing the rock away, the Grand Canyon is 4,000 feet deep and 277 miles long! Visitors can hike, raft or just take in the views.

Why?

Nature To-Do List

How many of these nature activities can you do?
Keep track as you check off
all the items on your nature to-do list.

➤ **See a waterfall**   Date: ....
  Location: ....

➤ **Swim in a lake**   Date: ....
  Location: ....

➤ **Hike a mountain**   Date: ....
  Location: ....

➤ **See a cactus**   Date: ....
  Location: ....

➤ **Climb a tree**   Date: ....
  Location: ....

➤ **Sleep under the stars**   Date: ....
  Location: ....

➤ **Roll down a hill**   Date: ....
  Location: ....

➤ **Observe the wildlife**   Date: ....
  Location: ....

➤ **Step into the ocean**   Date: ....
  Location: ....

Mother Nature's Marketing Team

Design a billboard advertising nature.
Think about what makes nature so great and
what might encourage people to spend more time
outside. Be sure to include eye-catching
art and a catchy slogan!

Rub It In!

Have you ever noticed the intricate patterns and textures that can be found in the natural world around us? From the rough bark of a tree to the veins of a leaf, texture is a really cool way to explore nature.

You can take a little bit of texture home with you by making your own rubbings!

Instructions

1. Find something like a leaf to use for your rubbing.

2. Place a piece of paper on top of your object of choice.

3. Using the side of a crayon or pencil, gently rub back and forth all over the object.

4. Admire your work!

Tape your rubbings here! Or use this page!

Nature Walk Scavenger Hunt

See how many of these objects you can spot in the great outdoors.

- ☐ Animal tracks
- ☐ Anthill
- ☐ Beetle
- ☐ Bird (Can you identify what species it is?)
- ☐ Bird's nest
- ☐ Butterfly
- ☐ Cloud
- ☐ Cool rock
- ☐ Feather
- ☐ Litter (Pick it up!)
- ☐ Mossy log
- ☐ Pine cone
- ☐ Seed pod
- ☐ Something shaped like a heart
- ☐ White flower
- ☐ Worm

Nature Games

These awesome activities will get you excited about the great outdoors.

Camouflage

Whoever is "it" closes their eyes and yells "Camouflage!" They count to 30 while everyone else runs and hides. On the count of 30, they open their eyes, and if they can spot anyone, they point and call them "out." In the next round, they yell "Camouflage!" and count to 10. Everyone who is not "out" must run toward them and re-hide. This continues until everyone is found or someone reaches the person who is "it" without being seen.

Animal Race

Make start and finish lines. One person is the judge and calls out the name of an animal and everyone must move like that animal from the start to the finish. Points for speed, accuracy and creativity of animal movement.

Oh, Snap!

One person closes their eyes and sits on the ground with a pile of sticks behind them. The rest sit in a line behind them and take turns trying to sneak up and get a stick. If the person hears a sound, they must point in the direction of who they think made it and that person must replace the stick. If they get back without being heard, they can keep the stick. When all the sticks are gone, whoever has the most is the winner.

Word Portrait

Can you create a "picture" of something in nature using words?

Draw the outline of something you see. Inside of your outline, write words that describe the item you see.
  Imagine you are painting a picture of what your object looks, feels and smells like, but using only words. Write down as many words as you can, then read your poem out loud using a dramatic voice!

DID YOU KNOW?

Trees can "talk" to each other by using a network of roots underground. They can send signals about upcoming threats like disease or dry spells and other trees can prepare themselves in advance.

Weather the Weather

When you are out in nature, it's important to pay attention to the weather so you don't get too cold or too hot.

Today's weather is:

 sunny

 windy

 cloudy

 rainy

Was the weather good for your activity today?

☐ Too hot   ☐ Too rainy   ☐ Just right

☐ Too cold   ☐ Too windy

What do you predict tomorrow's weather will be?

....

What do you hope it will be?

....

That Was Wild!

Reflect on your adventure
exploring the great outdoors.

What was one thing about today that surprised you?

....
....
....
....

Did you learn any new skills on this trip?

....
....
....
....

If you woke up as an animal tomorrow, what would you see and do?

. . . .

. . . .

. . . .

If the plants you saw today could speak, what do you think they would say to you?

. . . .

. . . .

. . . .

What do you think is the most important thing about being in nature?

. . . .

. . . .

. . . .

. . . .

What other nature adventures do you want to do?

. . . .

. . . .

. . . .

. . . .

A Day at the Beach

DATE

No matter what kind of beach you visit, it's sure to be a fun day. Pack your swimsuit, grab your sunscreen and head to the beach!

Where are you?

Who are you traveling with?

What type of beach are you visiting?

☐ **Ocean**   ☐ **Bay**   ☐ **Lake**   ☐ **River**

Using only 10 words, describe the beach you are visiting.

What did you bring with you to the beach today?

. . . .

Snacks taste better by the water. What would you pack for a picnic on the beach if you could choose from anything in the world?

. . . .

What do you like to wear when you go swimming? Do you wear goggles? Fins? Floaties? Is your swimsuit plain or does it have a bold pattern? Draw your beach outfit!

NO SUNBURNS HERE!

It's important to wear sunscreen when you're out in the sun. We measure how strong sunscreen is using a number called SPF. What do you think SPF might stand for? Write your guesses, then check the answer on pg. 109.

S . . . . P . . . . F . . . .

Busy at the Beach

Surf

How brave are you today?

Super brave → What do you like better?

Kind of brave → Jump in the water

Not very brave → Dip your toes in

Which do you prefer?

Yes → Do you like looking for buried treasure?

Sand

Are you OK getting sandy?

No → Time for beach reading

There's so much to do by the water, it's hard to fit it all in one day! Use this handy flowchart to figure out what activities you should try today!

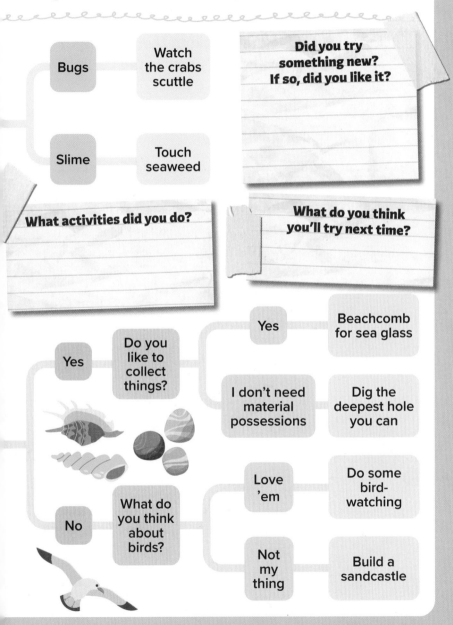

We See Seashells

Seashells are much more than cool beach treasures. They're also what tons of
sea creatures call home, making them an important part of the ocean's environment.

Can you figure out who lives in each shell? Draw a line to match the shell with the correct name!

A Clam ( )

B Whelk ( )

C Oyster ( )

D Scallop ( )

E Cowrie ( )

F Mussel ( )

G Conch ( )

Search the beach. Can you find any of these shells? Write down how many you can spot!

Answers on pg. 113

Feelin' Crabby

Hermit crabs find shells made by other creatures
and put them on like clothing!

**Do you think you'd like living in
a shell? Why or why not?**

. . . .

. . . .

. . . .

**If you chose a shell to wear like a hermit crab does,
what features would you look for?**

. . . .

. . . .

**Doodle Spot
Draw yourself as a hermit crab!**

Turn the Beach Into Your Game Board

Sand isn't just for sandcastles! A big stretch of blank sand can become your game board. Try out these games that you can play by writing and drawing in the sand, or try inventing your own. (Here's a secret: You can also play these games at home with sidewalk chalk!)

1. Giant Tic-Tac-Toe

Everyone knows tic-tac-toe, but have you ever played the GIANT version? Find a large patch of empty beach and draw a giant tic-tac-toe grid in the sand. Then, use your body to mark each move! You can run around in circles for O or make a sand angel for X. Get creative!

2. Contour Drawing

Try getting a little artsy and use the beach as your canvas. Pick something to draw, like someone else in your group or the sandwich you're about to eat. Using a stick, try to draw your subject in the sand using only one line (wet sand works a lot better for this!). If you want to get really funky with it, try doing the drawing using only your big toe!

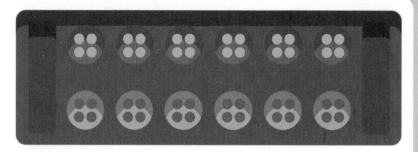

3. Mancala

Mancala is a very old game that's still popular today!
The goal of the two person game is to collect the most stones in your store.

Create your board: Each person digs six pits in front of them and one long one for your store at the end, like the image above.

Collect game pieces: Each person should find 18 pebbles, shells or other small game pieces. Put three into each pit in front of you.

Rules: On a turn, take all the pieces from any of your pits and, starting with the next pit to the right, add one piece to each pit until your hand is empty. If you come to your store, add one piece to your store, and continue to the other player's pits, moving counter-clockwise around the board, only skipping the other player's store. If your last piece ends in your store, you go again.

Ending the game: The game continues until all the pieces are in the stores. Whoever has the most pieces in their store wins.

4. X Marks the Spot

Play like a pirate! Find a special bit of treasure on the beach, like a nice shell, to be your buried treasure. Take turns secretly burying the treasure and marking the location with an X in the sand. Everyone else must try to find the buried treasure and bring it back! If you want, you can provide hints or draw a treasure map with directions to your hiding spot.

You're All Beached Out!

Aren't you glad you wore sunscreen?
Reflect on your day by the water.

What was your favorite part of this adventure?

What will you try on your next beach day?

How often would you like to come to the beach?
☐ every day ☐ once a month ☐ once a year ☐ NEVER!

If you were writing a book about your adventures, what would this chapter be titled?

What would the first sentence of the chapter be?

Pick It Up!

Trash, like plastic bags, straws and bottle caps, can harm the creatures who live on beaches and in the water. When you go home, make sure you take all your garbage with you. If you see any other garbage on the beach, be a hero and throw it out, too!

Draw any trash you collected today in the spaces below.

DATE

Eating in a Restaurant

Dining out can be quite the adventure.
Hope you're hungry!

Where are you?

Who are you traveling with?

Are you an adventurous eater or do you prefer to stick to foods you know you like?

What is your favorite food?

What is the worst food you've ever eaten?

Become a Food Explorer

A great way to experience a different culture or place is to try its food. You may have to be a little brave to try something that is very different from the type of food you are used to.

What was the food you tried called?

. . . .

What country is this food from?

. . . .

Where did you try it?

. . . .

Draw what it looks like.

Check all that apply. The food was:

☐ SPICY ☐ CRISPY ☐ MUSHY ☐ SOUR
☐ SWEET ☐ SALTY ☐ TANGY ☐ CHEWY

What did you think?

☐ I loved it!

☐ Hmm, I'd try it again.

☐ Not for me! Thanks but no thanks.

Restaurant Review

Some people's job is to go to restaurants and write a review of what they liked or didn't like. Sounds pretty great!
Can you be a reviewer for your restaurant?

Write a title for your restaurant review:

➤ Name of restaurant: ....

➤ Location: ....

➤ What did you order? ....

➤ Describe what you liked or didn't like. ....

....

....

➤ Part of going to a restaurant is the ambience (look and feel). How would you describe your restaurant's ambience? ....

....

....

➤ Give your restaurant a rating, 1 to 5 stars:

☆ ☆ ☆ ☆ ☆

A Pie by Any Other Name

Many cultures have some sort of pie: a sweet or savory filling surrounded by dough. Can you match the type of pie to the country or region it comes from?

A. Pumpkin Pie

B. Spanakopita

☐ 1. Australia
☐ 2. United States
☐ 3. Canada
☐ 4. Lebanon
☐ 5. Wales
☐ 6. Greece
☐ 7. South America

G. Pasty

C. Meat Pie

F. Empanada

E. Sfiha

D. Saskatoon Berry Pie

Answers on pg. 121

Tabletop Games

With good food and better company, there's no telling just how much fun you can have at the table!

What's Missing?
One person hides something from the table while everyone else's eyes are closed. Everyone opens their eyes and has to figure out what's missing.

Guess Who's Coming to Dinner?
Discreetly look at other diners and try to guess their names, where they live, what job they have and their biggest claim to fame. Let your imaginations run wild, but be courteous.

Straw Worms

Scrunch your paper straw wrapper to one end of the straw and remove it. Drop a tiny drop of water from the end of your straw onto the wrapper and watch your worm wriggle!

"Would You Rather?" Restaurant Edition

Take turns asking which of two foods you'd rather eat. For example, would you rather eat snails or octopus? Chocolate ice cream or cherry pie?

Story-Starter

One person starts a story and then it goes around the table and everyone adds one sentence to the story. You won't believe where things end up!

THE COMPANY YOU KEEP

Mealtime is a great time to connect with family and friends and share good stories. Can you make up a story to tell your tablemates? It can be something that happened to you that day or you can get creative and make up a funny story!

Find more tabletop games on *MommyPoppins.com*.

pg. 119 answers: **1.** C. Meat pie **2.** A. Pumpkin pie **3.** D. Saskatoon berry pie **4.** E. Sfiha **5.** G. Pasty **6.** B. Spanakopita. **7.** F. Empanada

Reviewer's Review

Now that you've sampled some tasty bites and tried your hand at being a food reviewer, review your experience!

Did you try any new foods? What did you think?

Invent your own dish. Give it a name and write how you would describe it on a menu.

WOULD YOU GO?
☐ **YES**   ☐ **NO**

If you like to see where your food comes from, you can't do much better than the Ithaa Undersea Restaurant in the Maldives. Dine under a glass dome 15 feet below the surface of the ocean while fish and sharks swim all around you. Just be glad it's the fish on the menu and not the other way around!

Draw or write down everything you put in your stomach today!

- . . . .
- . . . .
- . . . .
- . . . .
- . . . .
- . . . .
- . . . .
- . . . .
- . . . .
- . . . .
- . . . .

What surprised you about today's adventure?

. . . .
. . . .

What foods would you like to try next?

. . . .
. . . .

Groceries Galore

Whether you explore your regular grocery store, a farmer's market, a specialty food store or a market on your travels, shopping for food can make for a great adventure!

DATE

Where are you shopping today?

. . . .

Who are you with?

. . . .

. . . .

Is this your local grocery store or is it new to you?

. . . .

. . . .

What are you shopping for? Write your list here.

-
-
-
-
-
-
-
-
-
-
-
-
-

Be a Grocery Adventurer!

Discover a new ingredient! Check the produce section or the international foods aisle for something you've never tried before.

Draw your food item below.

What do you think it will taste like?

How do you think you prepare it?

What meals or snacks do you think you could make with it?

Ask your grown-up if you can make a recipe together using your ingredient!

Fun With Friends

Friendship is its own kind of adventure, whether you're hanging with old friends or making new ones.

Where are you?

....

Who are you with?

....

Friendship portrait (draw your friend's face below)

Name:

Age:

How long have you known each other?

Tell the story of how you met.

What's your favorite thing to do together?

Creative Collaboration

Working together can really push your creative limits. Try this artistic activity with a friend.

Take turns drawing a picture together, without talking at all. For an added challenge, you can set a timer for one minute for the first round, then 30 seconds, then 15 seconds, then five seconds.

In the Neighborhood

You don't have to travel far to have an adventure.
There's lots to discover right on your street.

Ask a Neighbor
Interview a neighbor to get a different perspective on your community.
What does your neighbor like about living here?

What is their happiest memory here?

What is their favorite place in the neighborhood?

How long have they lived here?

Have they ever lived anywhere else? If so, where?

Neighborhood Tour Guide

Do you have what it takes to give an insider's tour of your neighborhood?

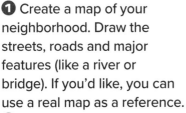

❶ Create a map of your neighborhood. Draw the streets, roads and major features (like a river or bridge). If you'd like, you can use a real map as a reference.

❷ Label interesting places and must-see attractions that you want to point out on your tour with a star. You might want to document a cool spider web or something historic. Talk to neighbors to find out any exciting facts or stories they have.

❸ Invite people to go on your tour and take them around, telling them the facts and stories you've collected for each of the starred spots.

☆	A	B	C	D	E	☆
1						
2						
3						
4						
☆						☆

It's All Relative

Turn family time into a fact-finding mission! What new things can you learn about the people you're related to?

Family Fact Finder

Quiz your relatives and fill in the chart with each person's answers. As you go, see if you can get them to tell you any funny stories behind the answers too!

Name			
Birth year			
Favorite color			
Childhood pet			
Favorite snack			
First job			
First celebrity crush			
Favorite movie as a kid			
Childhood hobby			

Family Treat

Fill out your family cake! Each layer of the cake is another generation of family members. Start with your generation (the kids!) at the top, then add your parent's generation (the grown-ups) in the next layer, and so on. If they feel like family, they belong in the cake. How many layers down can you go?

My Family

What's one thing about your family that you are most grateful for?

A Walk in the Park

Whether at home or abroad, there's so much to discover at the local park!

Walk the Alphabet
Can you find something for each letter of the alphabet as you explore? See how many you can fill in!

A ....

B ....

C ....

D ....

E ....

F ....

G ....

H ....

I ....

J ....

K ....

L ....

M ....

N ....

O ....

P ....

Q ....

R ....

S ....

T ....

U ....

V ....

W ....

X ....

Y ....

Z ....

Sometimes, adventuring means exploring the whole wide world, but looking super closely at one thing can be just as interesting. Pick a tree to zoom in on.

What species of tree is it? If you don't know, try to figure it out using a plant identifier app or book!

Draw the shape of the tree's leaves.

Is the bark rough or smooth? Do a bark rubbing to show the texture.

What bugs or animals can you spot living in or on the tree?

Write a poem about the tree.

How else does this tree help other creatures?

Movie Night

Movies are a way to explore
the world while staying cozy!

**What kind of movie watcher are you?
Check the one you prefer.**

✓	Movie theater	VS.	Couch	✓
✓	Chitchat	VS.	Quiet on set	✓
	Eyes on the screen	VS.	Asleep by the credits	✓
✓	Popcorn lover	VS.	Popcorn hater	✓

My Favorite Films
**List your favorite movies here.
What do you love about them?**

	Title	Reason(s)
1		
2		
3		

Cinema Bucket List

**Can you watch a movie from every category?
Write them down (along with your rating) below!**

Category	Title	Date watched	Stars
A movie about animals			☆☆☆☆☆
A movie you've seen over and over			☆☆☆☆☆
A movie in another language			☆☆☆☆☆
An animated movie			☆☆☆☆☆
A movie that takes place in another country			☆☆☆☆☆
A musical			☆☆☆☆☆

MY FIRST FILM

If you were going to make a movie, what would it be?

Title:

What is it about?

HOME SWEET HOME

Adventure Complete!

From point A to point Z and everywhere in between, you've seen, done and learned so much on your travels. Take a moment to soak it all in before it's time to hit the road all over again.

DATE

Are you excited to be back home? Why or why not?

What places and activities did you like best?

Write down one memory you'll never forget.

What are you most proud of doing or trying?

Does being home feel any different than it did before you left? Why or why not?

Who or what did you miss the most while on your travels?

What adventures do you want to try next?

Travel Badges

You became a better, smarter and stronger adventurer with every new trip under your belt.

What travel skills have you learned?
Write the date as you earn each badge.

Waited in a long line

Tried a new food

Didn't lose anything

DATE_____

DATE_____

DATE_____

Survived something stinky

Packed my own suitcase

Learned a new word

DATE_____

DATE_____

DATE_____

Saw something ancient

DATE_____

Had an attitude of gratitude

DATE_____

Walked for miles

DATE_____

Got up at dawn

DATE_____

Created a bucket list

DATE_____

Became an art lover

DATE_____

Became a history buff

DATE_____

Admired a beautiful sunset

DATE_____

Create your own badge!

DATE_____

Souvenir Spot

The best souvenirs help you remember how you felt while traveling. Even simple objects like a ticket stub, the label from a special snack or a photograph can make amazing souvenirs.

Tape or paste any souvenirs you've collected onto these pages.

About the Authors

Anna Fader and Amelia Eigerman are a mother-daughter team. Since 2007, when Anna started the website Mommy Poppins, their family has traveled extensively to discover the best destinations and activities for families and learned how to turn any day into an adventure. Anna and Mommy Poppins are recognized as leading authorities on family activities and travel, cited in publications including *The New York Times*, *The Washington Post* and *Forbes*, among others.

ANNA FADER is the founder and CEO of the acclaimed website Mommy Poppins, which inspires and helps families have more fun quality time together, with local guides and activity calendars in major U.S. cities and hundreds of destinations around the world.

AMELIA EIGERMAN grew up as the original "fun tester" for Mommy Poppins. This important job helped Amelia develop a love of travel and doing all the things. Now, Amelia is an emergency room veterinary technician. They use their science background to write about pets, wildlife and the climate for both kids and adults.

CONNECT

We'd love to hear from you!
Connect with Anna and Mommy Poppins on:
- **Facebook:** Mommy Poppins
- **Instagram:** @MommyPoppins
- **TikTok:** @MommyPoppins

Reach out to Amelia:
- **Instagram:** @EigermanWrites
- **X:** EigermanWrites

Media Lab Books
For inquiries, contact customerservice@topixmedia.com

PUBLISHED BY TOPIX MEDIA LAB
14 WALL STREET, SUITE 3C
NEW YORK, NY 10005

PRINTED IN CHINA

ISBN-13: 978-1-964487-01-4
ISBN-10: 1-964487-01-3

CEO Tony Romando

Vice President & Publisher Phil Sexton
Senior Vice President of Sales & New Markets Tom Mifsud
Vice President of Retail Sales & Logistics Linda Greenblatt
Vice President of Manufacturing & Distribution Nancy Puskuldjian
Digital Marketing & Strategy Manager Elyse Gregov

Chief Content Officer Jeff Ashworth
Senior Acquisitions Editor Noreen Henson
Creative Director Susan Dazzo
Photo Director Dave Weiss
Executive Editor Tim Baker
Managing Editor Tara Sherman

Content Editor Juliana Sharaf
Content Designer Mikio Sakai
Features Editor Trevor Courneen
Designers Glen Karpowich, Alyssa Bredin Quirós
Copy Editor & Fact Checker Madeline Raynor
Assistant Photo Editor Jenna Addesso
Assistant Managing Editor Claudia Acevedo